HIDDEN HISTORY
SPIES

Rose Greenhow

CONFEDERATE SPY

by Joanne Mattern
illustrated by Scott R. Brooks

RED
CHAIR
•PRESS•

Hidden History: Spies is produced and published by Red Chair Press:

Red Chair Press LLC   PO Box 333   South Egremont, MA 01258-0333

www.redchairpress.com

Publisher's Cataloging-In-Publication Data

Names: Mattern, Joanne, 1963- | Brooks, Scott R., 1963- illustrator.

Title: Rose Greenhow : Confederate spy / by Joanne Mattern ; illustrated by Scott R. Brooks.

Description: [South Egremont, Massachusetts] : Red Chair Press, [2018] | Series: Hidden history: spies | Interest age level: 008-012. | Includes sidebars of interest, a glossary, and resources to learn more. | Includes bibliographical references and index. | Summary: "No one expected Rose Greenhow to be a war hero. But when the American Civil War split the nation apart, this beautiful and popular hostess played an important role in the Confederate South's most important battle victory."--Provided by publisher.

Identifiers: LCCN 2017934024 | ISBN 978-1-63440-281-1 (library hardcover) | ISBN 978-1-63440-287-3 (ebook)

Subjects: LCSH: Greenhow, Rose O'Neal, 1814-1864--Juvenile literature. | Spies--United States--History--19th century--Juvenile literature. | United States--History--Civil War, 1861-1865--Secret service--Juvenile literature. | CYAC: Greenhow, Rose O'Neal, 1814-1864. | Spies--United States--History--19th century. | United States--History--Civil War, 1861-1865--Secret service.

Classification: LCC E608.G83 M38 2018 (print) | LCC E608.G83 (ebook) | DDC 973.78/6/0924--dc23

Photo credits: p. 4, 17, 20: Library of Congress; p. 32: Courtesy of the author, Joanne Mattern; p. 32: Courtesy of the illustrator, Scott R. Brooks

Map illustration by Joe LeMonnier

Printed in the United States of America

1117 1P CGBS18

Table of Contents

Chapter 1

A Secret Message

Rose Greenhow had a secret life. Most people knew her as a pretty, lively woman who hosted popular parties at her house in Washington, D.C. Rose had many close friends in the government. Her home was the center of Washington social life.

In 1861, the United States was torn apart by the Civil War. Rose lived in the North, but her heart was with the **Confederate** government in the South. Few people knew that Rose was not just a woman who liked to have friends over. She was really a Confederate spy!

Portrait of Rose Greenhow
between 1855 and 1865

The Nation Breaks Apart

During the 1850s, problems were building between the northern United States and the southern United States. The main issue was slavery. The North believed that slavery was wrong. They wanted to abolish, or get rid of, slavery.

Slavery in the North

Some well-known U.S. heroes such as John Hancock and Benjamin Franklin bought and sold slaves. Slave burial grounds have been discovered in Philadelphia and New York City.

People in the South had a different idea. They used slaves to work on their **plantations**. The South had an **agricultural** economy. Without slaves, their **economy** could not survive. Things were different in the North, which had an **industrial** economy.

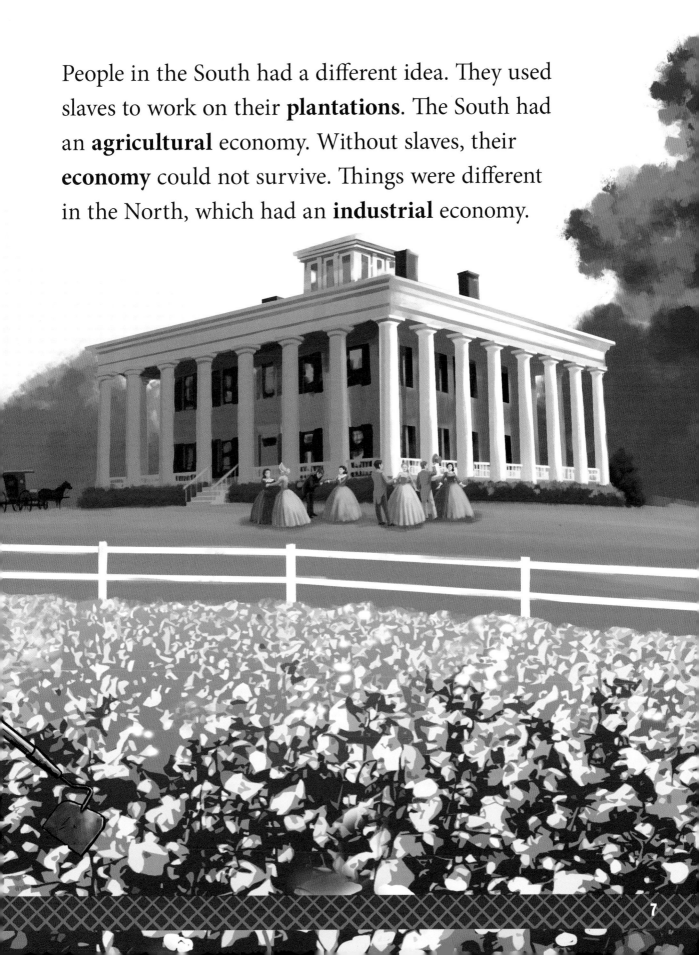

People in the South also believed that the **federal** government and the North should not be able to tell the South what to do. As the years passed, the argument got more violent. Finally, on April 12, 1861, the South left the United States. The Civil War had begun.

Rose lived in Washington. She knew many people in the government. She pretended to be loyal to the North, which was called the **Union**. When she gave parties, she listened to people talk. She learned many things.

The southern states broke from the United States to form a new Confederacy with capital in Richmond, VA.

In July 1861, Rose heard that the Union army was sending a lot of troops to Manassas, Virginia. She knew she had to get word to P.T. Beauregard, who was a general in the Confederate army.

Rose already knew a few things about spying and sending messages. She came up with a very clever plan.

Rose wrote a message in a secret code called a **cipher**. She gave it to a friend named Betty Duvall. Betty dressed up as a simple farm girl and rode a horse to Fairfax, Virginia. No one suspected who she really was or what she was doing.

When Betty reached the Fairfax County courthouse, she told an officer there that she had an urgent message for General Beauregard. When the officer agreed to give it to Beauregard, Betty unpinned her hair. As her long, thick hair came down, she pulled out a tiny package wrapped in silk. Inside was a note from Rose describing the Union army's plans.

Rose's secret information helped Beauregard win the Battle of Manassas. People in the South soon heard about Rose. They believed she was a hero. Beauregard and Confederate President Jefferson Davis both honored Rose when they met her.

Rose Greenhow went on to help the Confederacy in many ways. In just a few short years, she would live a life of adventure and daring. How did this woman become one of the South's boldest spies? Her life took many surprising turns along the way.

Chapter 2

Wife, Mother... and Slavery Supporter

Rose O'Neal was born around 1817 in Montgomery County, Maryland. She was such a lively girl that everyone called her "Wild Rose." Rose's parents died when she was very young. She went to live with an aunt who ran an inn and a school in Washington, D.C.

Rose made many friends. As she got older, she was very popular as well. She was always going to parties and having fun. Finally, in 1835, Rose married a young doctor and lawyer named Robert Greenhow.

Home, Sweet...Prison?

Rose's aunt's inn was in a building called the Old Capitol. Congress met there for a short time after the War of 1812. Later, the Old Capitol would become a prison—and Rose would be one of its prisoners!

The Greenhows lived in Washington, D.C. Robert worked for the government. The couple had many famous friends, including the President. Rose became especially close to a Southern politician named John C. Calhoun. Rose was already a supporter of slavery and the South, and so was Calhoun. The two became great friends.

No California?

As a Senator from South Carolina, John C. Calhoun opposed California's bid to join the U.S. as a free state.

The Greenhows had four daughters. They were Florence, Gertrude, Leila, and Rose, who was called "Little Rose." In 1854, Dr. Greenhow was killed in an accident while the family lived in San Francisco. Rose and her daughters moved back to Washington, D.C.

Rose's Hero

John C. Calhoun held many government positions, including senator, secretary of state, and vice president. After he died in 1850, Rose wrote, "I am a Southern woman, born with revolutionary blood in my veins, and my first crude ideas on State and Federal matters received consistency and shape from the best and wisest man of this century, John C. Calhoun."

John C. Calhoun

Chapter 3

Civil War Spy!

Soon after the Civil War began, Rose met a Confederate captain named Thomas Jordan. Jordan asked Rose to spy for him. He gave Rose a cipher so she could send him secret messages.

Rose was happy to spy for the Confederates. Because she knew so many powerful people in the federal government, she was able to find out many important things. One of these things was the upcoming Union attack on Manassas. Rose was able to send word to Confederate General P.T. Beauregard in time for him to gather his army and win the battle.

A Battle by Another Name

The Confederates called the battle Manassas. The Union called it the Battle of Bull Run.

Secret Ciphers

The cipher Rose used contained 26 symbols. Each symbol stood for a number, and each number stood for a letter. Rose wrote her messages in this secret code. The messages could then be read by Jordan or another Confederate officer who knew the code.

The federal government suspected Rose was a spy. They asked Allan Pinkerton to watch her. Pinkerton placed Rose and her daughter, Little Rose, under arrest in their home. Other spies were also held prisoner in Rose's house. The home soon became known as "Fort Greenhow."

Rose Greenhow with her daughter Rose, in the Old Capitol Prison

From Secret Agent to Detective

Allan Pinkerton went on to start a famous detective agency that he named after himself.

Pinkerton went through Rose's letters. He found proof that Rose was sending information to the South. Even though Pinkerton was watching her, Rose still found ways to send information. She used secret words that gave clues to her Southern friends. She also fooled Pinkerton into thinking she was using invisible ink. Pinkerton was so busy trying to discover invisible writing that he did not notice clues Rose wrote in plain sight!

Finally, in January, 1862, Rose and Little Rose were sent to the Old Capitol Prison. Even in jail, Rose still sent messages! She placed candles in her window as symbols. Other spies could see them and figure out the message Rose was sending. Rose also sent messages through letters to friends and visitors.

Rose and her daughter were let out of prison in May. They were brought to Virginia and told to stay behind Confederate lines. Rose was welcomed as a hero in the South. Rose later wrote that the proudest moment of her life came when Confederate President Jefferson Davis thanked her for helping the South win the Battle of Manassas.

Poor Rose

Southern newspapers wrote articles complaining that the Union was cruel to put a mother and her young daughter in jail. These articles made Rose even more famous and helped Southerners admire her even more.

President Davis asked Rose to go to Europe. She could tell important people there about the South. She would get money and support for their side of the war. At that time, there was a **blockade** to prevent ships from sailing between the Confederate States and Europe. Rose did not care. She boarded a ship and made it to England.

Rose spent the next year traveling around England and France. She met Queen Victoria of England. Many wealthy and important people in Europe supported the South. Rose made many friends and was an important figure there, just as she had been in Washington.

Rose the Writer

Rose wrote a book while she was in England. It was called *My Imprisonment and the First Year of Abolition Rule at Washington*. The book became a best-seller in England.

Chapter 4

A Shocking Death

Rose set sail for America in August 1864. She carried important **documents** from England's government. She also carried $2,000 worth of gold coins sewn into her dress. She planned to give the money to the Confederacy.

On October 1, the ship reached the North Carolina coast. A Union gunboat began chasing it. Rose's ship ran aground. Rose did not want to get caught, so she jumped into a rowboat. But the water was rough, and the rowboat tipped over. Rose could not swim because of all the heavy gold she was carrying in her gown. Weighed down by the gold, Rose drowned.

Rose was buried with full **military** honors in North Carolina. Six months later, in April 1865, the Union won the Civil War. Rose is still remembered today as a brave and daring woman who worked hard to help the people she loved. Her courage and charm are admired even by people who fought on the other side of the war.

MRS ROSE O.N. GREENHOW
A BEARER
OF DISPATCHES
TO THE
CONFEDERATE GOVERNMENT

Erected by the Ladies
Memorial association

Glossary

abolition a movement to end slavery

agricultural having to do with farming

blockade sealing off a place to prevent people and goods from leaving or entering

cipher a secret way of writing

Confederate having to do with the 11 Southern states that left the Union between 1861 and 1865

documents important papers

economy the wealth and resources of a place

federal having to do with central government

industrial having to do with making goods in factories

military having to do with the armed forces

plantations large farms where crops such as cotton and tobacco are grown

Union the states that remained loyal to the federal government during the Civil War; the North

For More Information

Books About the Civil War

Cummings, Judy Dodge. *Civil War Leaders*. Abdo Publishing, 2016.

George, Enzo. *The Civil War*. Cavendish Square Publishing, 2015.

Grayson, Robert. *12 Incredible Facts about the U.S. Civil War*. 12-Story Library, 2016.

Kolpin, Molly. *Great Women of the Civil War*. Capstone, 2015.

Shattuck, Jason. *The Civil War*. Rosen Publishing, 2016.

Books About Spies

Hyde, Natalie. *Classified: Spies at Work*. Crabtree Publishing Company, 2015.

Polansky, Daniel. *War Spies*. Scholastic, 2013.

Sodaro, Craig. *Civil War Spies*. Velocity, 2014.

Places

Manassas National Battlefield Park, Manassas, Virginia

Rose O'Neal Greenhow Burial Site, Wilmington, North Carolina

Index

About the Author and Illustrator

Joanne Mattern is the author of many nonfiction books for children. She enjoys writing about animals, history, and famous people while bringing history to life for young readers. Joanne lives in New York State with her husband, four children, and several pets.

Scott R. Brooks started a career in full-time illustration several years ago. Scott shares his Atlanta, GA studio with his illustrator wife, Karen. They share their home with their 2 clever children, and their somewhat less clever dog and cat.